What Our Readers Have Said...

Applicability

"These books are great tools that should be used as guidelines for our everyday supervisory practices. You need to take the time to do a short self-evaluation when reading them."

•

"The Pinpoint Training Series delivers information that could be used in a lot different areas."

•

"The things and problems we deal with everyday are discussed in these books."

Convenience

"I like this because I can take them with me to read at a convenient time. I feel the little time I have to spend in the office is best use on activities that directly relate to revenue opportunities. I like the short amount of time it takes to keep up with these."

•

"I prefer the self-study approach; it fits in with my schedule."

•

"I like the fact that the format allows the books to be reviewed as time permits. All work has been conducted on personal, evening/weekend time."

•

"Easy to use... if you put the time into it."

Challenge

"My thought is that the real value of these books comes into effect when doing the action plans."

•

"I like the fact that the format allows assignments to be reviewed as time permits."

Clarity

"Short and sweet. These books are easy to comprehend."

•

"Easy to use, understand, and reference if needed."

Relevance

"I have enjoyed reading these books. They are relevant to today's work environment and the ongoing change in the way we manage our workforce."

•

"I believe the contents of the Pinpoint series are excellent. It causes one to reflect on the daily dynamics in working with oneself as well as with management and peers."

Creating & Sustaining a Strong Vision

Pinpoint Leadership Skill Development Training Series

TIMOTHY F. BEDNARZ

MAJORIUM
BUSINESS PRESS

Pinpoint Leadership Skill Development Training Series
"Creating & Sustaining a Strong Vision"
Timothy F. Bednarz

Graphic design: Monika Pawlak

Majorium Business Press
2025 Main Street
Stevens Point, WI 54481
715.342.1018 • 800.654.4935

ISBN 978-1-882181-38-4

Printed in the United States of America

Introduction

The Pinpoint Leadership Skill Development Training Series is designed for targeted training and education regarding increased improvement in a specific skill or competency.

Each book within this series is designed to be easy to use, understand and apply to your job. It can be used as a basis for training individuals, as a discussion guide or as a personal training tool.

Each chapter within this book discusses a specific concept. When you have completed all eight chapters you should have a 360° perspective of the topic.

Additionally, each chapter is divided into specific sections:

- The first section provides you with an overview of the topic
- The Implications section discusses why the concept is important, and why it is important to learn and apply.
- The Strategies, Tips & Techniques to Apply section teaches how to use and apply the particular concept to your work.
- The Points to Ponder section gives you something to think about or to be discussed with a group setting. These are questions not meant to be immediately answered, but to be pondered over time.
- The Training Activity section provides you with the tools to transfer what you have learned to your job. It is designed to help create an action plan to effectively apply the concept.

Each of the topics in this series is time-tested and proven in the marketplace. They have been used by thousands of employees as training tools. Many of the users have commented that what made these books valuable, was the ability to refer to them when a problem surfaced. They indicated that they remembered reading about the exact problem. They referred back to these books and found an appropriate solution.

You will find them equally valuable as a resource in your professional development library.

Table of Contents

LEARNING OBJECTIVES:

- To identify and apply the elements, factors and principles that define one's leadership vision.
- To interpret and analyze the critical factors and benefits of leadership vision.
- To identify the implications and ramifications of leadership vision that either enhances or diminishes its attainment.
- To apply specific strategies to enhance leadership vision and attainment.
- To understand and identify the negative consequences of failing to develop and maintain personal and organizational leadership vision.
- To analyze the expected results and outcomes of developing and maintaining leadership vision.

1

Leaders Have a Vision

Leaders are continually facing situations of constant change and adaptation. Creating and implementing a vision helps them determine ways to overcome associated roadblocks, hindrances and employee resistance.

As employees and leaders alike are typically subjected to a broad range of external and internal pressures, leaders are faced with the challenge of creating an appropriate or "right" vision, then persuading various categories of employees—from avid supporters to procrastinators and laggards—to accept the vision and work toward its fulfillment.

A carefully crafted leadership vision provides the means to generate new and more flexible ways of working and thinking as a group. It enables leaders to set a specific organizational course of direction, then pursue it by selecting, equipping and training employees focused on the mission and its objectives to carry it out.

IMPLICATIONS – WHAT THIS MEANS TO YOU

Defining, selling and emphasizing the vision motivates employees to willingly and enthusiastically expend personal, emotional, and physical energy in its pursuit. Specific organizational goals and objectives are accepted and embraced because employees have "bought in" to the vision.

A leader achieves this needed influence by displaying a servant attitude and modest stance while conveying a "prophetic and profound vision of the future." The vision and its associated direction are presented in clear terms that resonate with employee beliefs and values. Once this takes place, employees begin to understand and interpret "the future" in the context of present actions and steps.

During the process, the leader presents his or her vision in contrast to the present status and state of the organization. Through the use of critical thinking skills, insight, intuition, active listening and positive discourse, the leader is able to facilitate and draw out employee opinions and beliefs.

This process allows employees to move from ambiguity toward clarity of understanding, which helps them to develop shared insights that result in influencing them to see the future state of the organization as a desirable condition worth committing to.

STRATEGIES, TIPS & TECHNIQUES TO APPLY

The leader begins to move the vision forward in an ethical and productive way, which implies seeking out what constitutes "the greater good" in regard to his or her employees.

During this process the leader constantly emphasizes how and why the employees will be better off as a result of open and positive leadership interaction. The leader is then able to achieve higher levels of trust and commitment to the vision as he or she seeks personal growth, renewal, and increased stamina through these positive leader-employee interactions.

A Visionary Leader Is Set Apart from Others

Visionary leaders are in a different class than traditional mission-focused leaders.

They seem to sense the unknowable, which includes seeing others' unique talents and abilities. These tend to influence the decisions the leader makes, and help him or her shape a better plan for the future.

Leaders with vision are outstanding "conceptualizers," nurturing their own and others' abilities to dream and think beyond the ordinary and day-to-day limitations. They motivate across generational boundaries to enable employee groups to learn and embrace change.

As individual work environments often directly affect employee capabilities, visionary leaders know they can and should affect employee perceptions as to their own personal capabilities. An outcome of this process is that the leader can more fully prepare and build employee followers to accomplish what they are capable of and beyond. The building up of employee followers results in the leader knowing their capabilities to the point where enhanced trust empowers them to accomplish necessary organizational tasks, assignments and projects.

Visionary Leaders Are Motivators

Leaders with vision are extremely capable of motivating and instilling a sense of vision "buy-in," desire, commitment and determination in their employees. They have the innate ability to engage others in their direction. They also tend to be masters of determining their employees' true capacities, which can be used to help seek out and overcome optimal challenges.

Inspiring the vision implies rallying employees to acknowledge a common purpose and path of direction in its behalf. Employees become motivated to behave in particular, positive ways. This true sense of motivation does not spring from external rewards or threats, but internally from individual desires of job and personal satisfaction. Intrinsic motivation results in generating a sense of pleasure while interacting with others as well as while engaged in necessary jobs, projects and tasks.

Becoming a More Visionary Leader

Visionary leaders tend to transcend organizational expectations as well as the goals they set for themselves and their employees.

Leaders can become more forward-thinking, craft an inspiring vision and make it a reality by adhering to the following tips and strategies:

- Generate movement by focusing on what is in the best interests of their employees from a long-term standpoint.

- Motivate employees into action and commitment by satisfying their basic human needs.
- Talk in terms of dreams and possibilities that work to inspire the vision.
- Think in terms of a broader organizational view, as well as why it is important to forge a new territory of organizational direction.
- Remain farsighted while working in shorter steps that focus on generating small successful outcomes.
- Work to inspire employees to do things without actually sitting on top of them with a checklist in hand.
- Integrate employee ideas to foster ownership in the vision.
- Maintain the ability to see objectively and in an unbiased manner.
- Do the right thing in all circumstances and situations.
- Keep up with future trends and how they will effect the organization.
- Make consistent and effective contributions to work tasks and team projects.
- Continually inspire employee followers through speeches and pep talks that get them to work toward the vision.

POINTS TO PONDER – SOMETHING TO THINK ABOUT

1. Have you mentally created a larger organizational picture that includes your personal vision?
2. If you have crafted this organizational picture, what does it look like and how does it reflect your personal vision?
3. What things do you do to enhance the quality of your employees' work life in order to make them more active supporters of your vision and more motivated to work toward it?

TRAINING ACTIVITY – APPLICATION & ACTION PLAN

Revisit your vision and its direction. Using the following suggestions below, begin to redefine it if necessary. Determine ways to emphasize and promote it to your employees and other organizational members.

1. Instill a purpose and goal for the vision that reflects "what's in it" for your employees.
2. Create and establish a departmental and organizational philosophy that revolves around your vision. Promote it daily and apply any employee ideas, specific courses of action and implementation strategies reflecting it.
3. Describe your vision as well as its direction and associated expectations from multiple perspectives.
4. Communicate a short- range and long-range purpose for your vision.
5. Craft small incremental goals that can be reached in shorter periods of time to instill a sense of success and accomplishment.
6. Consistently provide the organization with a clear direction while outwardly motivating employees when they go through various challenges and changes.

2

Vision Is Essential

Napoleon once remarked, "Leaders are dealers in hope." Adapted to the corporate environment, this statement might read, "Vision is the faith by which the leader functions."

Leadership vision is one of the major characteristics defining a leader's identity and, in the end, reputation. Trust in one's leader and his or her vision enhances positive leadership outcomes, including overall improved job performance, job satisfaction, and organizational commitment.

A leader should generate a vision similar to that which inspires his or her employees in terms of clarity, challenge, and future orientation and inspiration. Employees need to be encouraged to share the leader's vision and use it to guide their daily operations. The leader should motivate and empower employees to pursue and attain the vision set before them.

IMPLICATIONS – WHAT THIS MEANS TO YOU

The question employees typically find themselves asking when a leader begins to define and implement action steps to attain his or her visions is: "Can we trust you not to abuse the privilege of authority?"

Credibility as a leader ultimately depends upon perceived vision-related integrity—namely, keeping one's word and commitment, not taking advantage of personal influence or authority, or manipulating employees into embracing the vision the leader wishes to attain.

Leaders able to maintain a persistent belief in their vision are further considered extremely competent by their employees and seen as a contributing resource rather than force to be opposed.

STRATEGIES, TIPS & TECHNIQUES TO APPLY

The depth and detail of a leader's vision demonstrates his or her level of expertise. Expertise is needed for legitimacy, employee respect and making the vision a reality.

As leaders are involved in decision making all day long, the quality of their decisions is compounded over time. Effective leaders who stand by their personal vision generally make prompt, wise and accurate decisions, even under unimaginably difficult and confusing conditions and situations.

Having a higher level of expertise makes a leader become very pragmatic. The leader tends to see things in realistic terms, which helps to identify and develop strategies that are able to cut through to the core of problems and negative situations relatively quickly. This aids in quicker vision realization.

Expertise is acknowledged and respected when a leader effectively projects his or her vision by explaining to employees the purpose, meaning and significance.

In addition to demonstrating decisiveness and expertise, clearly defining the vision and adhering to it serves the leader by enhancing team performance, generating healthy conflict, and driving overall change.

Enhanced Team Performance

Defining a vision through clarifying roles, goals, and the way forward is a proven means of increasing team performance.

The quality of the relationships employees develop (and the people with whom they develop them) is influenced to a large degree by inward assumptions about their leader's vision. When those assumptions are based on faulty generalizations, misunderstandings or misinterpretations, the quality of employee relationships suffers.

Factors that contribute to forming strong relationships across differences are affected by individual sets of experiences, beliefs and expectations. Vision has the power to generate positive experiences with others and realistic expectations of them. It helps to develop and maintain positive social identities through a process of molding individuals into a unified collaborative unit that shares the same beliefs, goals and outlooks.

In essence, if properly communicated and then embraced, vision positively shapes the way employees and leaders interact with one another. It helps to generate a type of "social identity" or a perception of oneness through shared and valued personal and work-related characteristics and goals.

Vision Generates Healthy Conflict

A visionary leader is often viewed as one who makes up his or her mind, then remains intractable and unmovable in direction and expectations. This perception tends to generate conflict and resistance.

The extent to which conflict emerges is dependent upon two factors: the strength of the visional expectation, or agreement between employees' perceptions of the steps needed to attain the vision and the leader's own expectations, and the outward attitudes, expressions, or behaviors the employee and leader display in embracing the vision and its directional courses of action.

When the two factors above are addressed, where persuasion and a sense of purpose and positive self-benefit are emphasized, feelings of harmony and balance typically replace levels of uncertainty, insecurity and resistance.

When leaders experience conflict, their ability to reduce or eliminate it will always depend upon how well they communicate their expectations both initially and over time.

Vision Drives Organizational Change

The need for change is normally stimulated by an external "trigger" necessitating a modification of some kind. Connecting the vision to this needed change typically forces the organization out of its status quo, alters values and attitudes, and establishes balance and stability.

Acceptance of change and related implementation procedures is loaded with human-related difficulties. Vision enables leaders to achieve higher levels of "buy in" by overcoming employees' anxiety over changes, their personal uncertainty and lack of ownership of initiatives and their outcomes.

Leaders understand the culture and capabilities of their organization, and use it as the basis for the embracement of visional change. This change is further effected by:

- Selecting key employees who tend to display unique leadership qualities to be project facilitators or unit directors for various assignments or tasks.
- Working with small groups of employees and mentoring them in various assignments and tasks as it relates to their visional impetus and direction.
- Creating ways for those involved in the change to share successes and failures.
- Using discussion group cycles or brainstorming to move their visional direction and strategic objectives forward.
- Developing small-scale achievable targets in order to introduce change or build small successes from them.
- Encouraging both themselves and their employees to be innovative as well as to engage in more productive behaviors in the workplace.
- Managing change proactively, by focusing forward movement on implementation and action rather than formal competence building.

POINTS TO PONDER – SOMETHING TO THINK ABOUT

1. Do you feel employees view you as "making up your mind and sticking to it" regarding organizational direction? Why or why not?
2. Do you see clearly defining and holding to your vision as helping develop and maintain positive social identities that allow employees to share similar beliefs, goals and outlooks? Why or why not?

TRAINING ACTIVITY – APPLICATION & ACTION PLAN

Look at your vision from the perspective of clarifying employee roles and related goals that move changes and projects forward. Begin to think of ways to help all employees work collaboratively toward a common vision-related goal. Write them down. Once this is determined, incorporate elements into their jobs and tasks that will help to cement together and unify them.

1. Monitor how productively they work as a group and observe how often they share various portions of work-related responsibilities.
2. "Talk and walk" your vision. Generate positive experiences with others in regard to it.
3. Identify factors that contribute to forming strong relationships and positive vision-centered experiences, beliefs, and expectations. Use them as much as possible to motivate and inspire.
4. Make certain that employee vision-related assumptions are not faulty, misunderstood or misinterpreted. If they appear to be, hold discussions to correct them.

3

Vision Is Essential to Decision Making

Employees share a leader's vision and use it to guide their daily operations. This is a key component of visionary leadership. Equally important are the specific characteristics of the shared vision and their impact on organizational performance.

Many organizations regard "vision setting" as the most crucial of all leadership tasks because the process enables them to survive and remain competitive. Without competent, vision-led leaders, employees have no motivational thrust to flame their passions, example to follow or compass to guide them.

However, a vision needs to be passionately shared between leaders and employees to make a positive impact on organizational performance. Fostering an acceptance of group goals generates a deepened desire among employees to work together toward a common goal.

To attain the organizational vision, leaders and employees need to depend upon one another. Without employee buy-in, leaders are faced with a solo effort—and limited prospects for success.

Essential to defining a vision is an understanding that leaders need to appreciate and articulate their "shared vision of the future."

IMPLICATIONS – WHAT THIS MEANS TO YOU

A vision needs to be shared before it can be attained. In defining a vision, the process needs to address specific action steps that inspire employee buy-in and ensure its attainment.

Leaders need to first consider critical vision-related factors from various viewpoints, and determine elements that are most important to incorporate as part of their visional direction.

The best place to start is to make certain the vision reflects the most effective ways to:

- Inject a purpose into collective employee and leader efforts;
- Create a departmental and organizational philosophy that revolves around visional ideas, implementation strategies and specific courses of action;
- Describe the vision from multiple perspectives;
- Establish a short- and long-range purpose;
- Consistently provide the organization with a clear direction, while outwardly motivating employees as they go through various challenges, transformations, conflict and turmoil.

Failing to create and proclaim an effective vision is a major reason why many corporate leaders and their change initiatives/programs fall far short of expectations and the vision's realization.

In addition to creating and sharing the vision, leaders must motivate and empower their employees. The manner in which leaders motivate and empower employees to achieve and sustain the shared vision, and followers' use of it, will in essence determine overall organizational performance. Employee followers are expected to use the vision to guide their daily operations, tasks and activities.

STRATEGIES, TIPS & TECHNIQUES TO APPLY

Vision is critical to organizational change and the various strategies that allow it to occur. It is often considered the impetus for enabling an organizational culture to implement changes—one of the responsibilities leaders are expected to fulfill.

Vision tends to be the organization's image of the future; defining it becomes the force behind shaping and framing meaning and purpose for all employees within the organization. While terms such as mission, goals, beliefs and organizational philosophy tend to differ from the actual interpretation of vision, they play a significant role in defining it.

As defining vision tends to depend upon individual leadership styles and interpretations, leaders need to develop a vision in their own way from an intuitive and subjective standpoint. Once identified, it guides his or her choices and actions.

Vision Defies a Single Definition

Defining "vision" and then actively sharing it has been widely regarded as a key to generating superior performance. Yet it is difficult to assign one meaning to the term as leaders typically use various techniques to entice and induce employees to act in a positive and forward-thinking manner.

A personal vision derives its power from its connection to key organizational initiatives, and from the leader's personal investment in seeing it come to fruition. Effective definition aligns the visions of leaders and employees, leading to a mutual sharing and commitment toward it.

A leader's vision must inspire employees to act on behalf of something that goes beyond their self-interests. Its power is a motivational force that engages employees in a shared quest to accomplish the extraordinary, not merely reach an expected productivity goal.

An effectively defined vision incorporates details that outline individual leaders' contributions to the organization. These can include modeling techniques, goal setting structures, rewards and/or punishments, reorganization, team-building and explicit ways to communicate the vision.

Vision Attributes and Content

In defining a vision, attributes and content should be similar, since both tend to reflect a common future direction between leaders and employees.

An effective vision needs to be inspiring, abstract, motivating, widely accepted and integrated with the visions of others. It is brief, yet clearly encompasses all of the necessary components that express its purpose and direction.

Strategic visions create the ability for a leader to interact to create positive performance. Content may focus on specific products, services, markets, organizational growth or even ideals. In order to identify an innovative competitive position, successful strategic visions also tend to take into account industry segments, customers, and the organization's specific competitive environment.

POINTS TO PONDER — SOMETHING TO THINK ABOUT

1. What does the term "shared vision" imply in terms of needed actions to support employee buy-in?
2. Can you think of ways to make a vision brief, yet clear in encompassing its purpose and direction?
3. How do you think a vision can be used to guide employees as well as day-to-day operations?

TRAINING ACTIVITY — APPLICATION & ACTION PLAN

When creating your vision think about how you intend to guide it to maintain acceptance and motivation towards its attainment. Begin by identifying a sense of structure that aids in its forward movement

1. Detail ways to offer guidance through a sense of inspiring a shared vision.
2. Identify how to effectively share the vision's "big picture."
3. Determine ways to best apply employee abilities and talents that will inspire them to accept and embrace a sense of ownership of the vision.
4. Work the vision into a contextual framework that employees can easily understand and embrace.

5. Detail actions and procedures where structures and systems within department(s) and the organization are able to reflect the vision.
6. Define and redefining your vision's sense of purpose and the reasoning behind it.

4

Overcoming Resistance to the Vision

Vision transcends organizational accomplishments, since visionary leaders tend to make a deep internal commitment to "doing the right thing" over "doing things right." This emphasis effectively works to overcome resistance to their vision.

Overcoming resistance requires that leaders continually make it a point to do the right thing in all circumstances. Leaders can sometimes expect to contend with immediate crises that place them in direct opposition to existing and traditional business logic, structures and norms.

Doing the right thing requires a leader's courage and personal commitment to core values, which includes placing everyone involved as a top priority.

IMPLICATIONS – WHAT THIS MEANS TO YOU

Promoting greater in-depth understanding of the "big picture" is essential to overcoming resistance. Implementing and working toward one's vision while reducing employee resistance implies acknowledging and embracing something larger that transcends personal self-interests. Attaining a vision requires thinking and acting in unconventional ways. This may open leaders up to criticism or other attacks.

Identifying and implementing vision depends upon the application of knowledge, intelligence and experience. How these three elements are linked and leveraged determines whether or not the vision is attained.

STRATEGIES, TIPS & TECHNIQUES TO APPLY

Vision components need to be interrelated, with all employees working cooperatively to promote positive outcomes that define its direction and movement toward success.

Lack of persistence, buy-in, motivation or collaborative thinking and action leads to resistance on all levels. The vision is relegated to an elusive dream incapable of achieving what leaders have set their sights on: anticipating and preempting problems, capitalizing on potential opportunities, mobilizing and engaging employees, and transforming their organizations from reactive to proactive workplaces.

Strategies for Overcoming Resistance

In order to reduce the likelihood of resistance from the onset, leaders need to overcome their biases, comfort zones and long-held beliefs. Being consistently non-judgmental and having a tolerance for ambiguity and uncertainty are two key leadership traits that must be employed and sustained if one's vision is to be realized.

To eliminate resistance on all fronts, leaders need to strive for creating positive cultural and workplace norms, structures and practices that promote analyzing and revising beliefs and assumptions in regard to visional acceptance and direction, which typically is a difficult task to accomplish.

Resistance is created because most employees prefer to cling to that which is known and comfortable rather than experience the discomfort of changing thinking and action. At this point leaders need to resist their conscious or unconscious need to assert power over others, since it will end up producing further resistance to vision acceptance and movement.

Five Major Areas Influencing Resistance

Five major factors influence whether levels of resistance are broken down in a positive way.

- Seeing the big picture from an organizational standpoint and separating details from principles or trends as well as symptoms from problems and their causes to identify and address the few issues and factors that really matter.
- Understanding the complexity of problems and situations, particularly from multiple viewpoints and through the eyes of senior management and other stakeholders.
- Recognizing personal limits, including the inability to see reality as it is, but as being tainted by past experiences, biases, prejudices and perceptions. These affect apprehending the true nature, implications, possibilities and consequences of vision-related realities.
- Making effective decisions and following them up with actions that work to promote the greater good.
- Leaders continually minimizing self-interests, and promoting and adhering to the value of honesty, especially when circumstances challenge and encourage a deviation from these principles.

Appreciation for Complexity and the Need for Systemic Thinking

Creating an awareness that problems are not simple is essential for viewing the realities of what is necessary to overcome them. Effective solutions to complex problems require leaders as well as employees to become systemic thinkers.

The more everyone knows about and understands the complex factors associated with particular challenges, the more they tend to be adaptable and creative in problem solving.

Thinking systemically begins with the realization that any problem is an integral part of a larger context. The more leaders and employees accept that situations are complex, the more equipped they become to deal with related problems.

Systemic thinking in problem solving includes identifying and working with relationships and the interdependencies among various interconnected elements.

Responses to problems often tend to attack the most painful symptoms attached to them. Immediately leaders and their employees, as an emotional reaction, search for and select remedies that on the surface seem to offer immediate relief for symptoms. This leads everyone into what is known as a "denial of complexity." When this takes root, some relief may be temporarily achieved, but the underlying cause for the existing problem(s) remains.

Vision Requires Sound Strategy and Action

Decision making and planning are needed before effective actions can be carried out, but will only be effective if placed into specific vision-related contexts.

Decision making and planning techniques may be analytical, thorough, and methodical, but they may not be effective in identifying the best course of action to reach and attain a leader's vision.

Values play a large part in this; for example if a leader accepts stewardship over his or her organizational department, then long-term consequences and sustainability will more likely than not tend to become more obvious and focused upon than any types of short-term profits, comfort or ease.

Another example is the decision by a leader to invest in developing people and creating a supportive work environment as part of ongoing vision-related initiatives.

Adopting a team-based approach to continuous improvement can be expected to drain resources as well as the time required to produce dividends. Yet expending these resources is a sound investment, as employees will be able to use new skills and aptitudes on future projects.

POINTS TO PONDER — SOMETHING TO THINK ABOUT

1. In what ways has overcoming vision resistance required you to do the right thing when something inwardly told you not to?
2. How do you personally interpret the term "denial of complexity"?
3. Within particular situations or problem solving encounters with employees, have you ever found yourself or others in a state of denial of complexity? If so, what was the result?

TRAINING ACTIVITY — APPLICATION & ACTION PLAN

Seeing the big picture from a personal as well as organizational standpoint is necessary to attain one's vision. To do this effectively, prepare ways to develop discussions with your employees regarding how to:

1. Understand the complexity of your vision-related problems and situations, particularly from multiple viewpoints and through the eyes of upper management and stakeholders.
2. Appropriately recognize and respond to personal limits of knowledge and insight. Discuss how these are continually tainted by past experiences, biases, prejudices and perceptions, and how they impact the nature, implications and possibilities of vision-related realities.
3. Make more effective decisions and follow them up with actions that work to serve and promote the greater good within the workplace.
4. Promote and adhere to the value of honesty, even when situations and challenges entice a deviation from the principle.

5

Developing Visionary Thinking

Leaders have a responsibility to connect elements of their vision in the context of thinking, planning and actions. Connecting vision to action and then to expected results depends upon effectively applying "visionary thinking" practices and principles. Visionary thinking then provides the means for strategic direction and specific deployment actions.

Leaders need to define the larger picture of who the organization is, which defines its being, and what it does, or its mission. This also includes identifying what values are important to the organization, where it is going or its visional direction, and why it must go in the direction its leaders determine. It takes visionary thinking to develop necessary strategies, procedures and plans capable of linking these elements in a way that moves employees and the organization forward.

It is no accident that visionary leaders generally become an organization's best teachers and create definite linkages between values, vision and mission. They make communication the cornerstone of the organizational culture, and inspire members to embrace, actively work toward and successfully attain the shared vision.

IMPLICATIONS – WHAT THIS MEANS TO YOU

The need for organizational change and sometimes a new course or direction is often not clear to management and/or the workforce. Visionary thinking works to integrate a strategic direction of an organization to a long-term destination, which then sets into motion various key elements and processes that work together to effect necessary changes. From a visionary standpoint, it is the leader's primary responsibility to set the context for needed changes and present compelling reasons why management and employees alike should accept the challenges that the changes represent.

If the need for vision-related change is not clearly communicated in an organization's strategic direction, then the value of planned strategies, goals, objectives, as well as the vision driving the intended changes will ultimately come into question. If the rationale behind particular changes is not thoroughly understood, the changes will be resisted. Then either nothing happens, or employees will only demonstrate superficial compliance.

STRATEGIES, TIPS & TECHNIQUES TO APPLY

Leadership is defined by recognizing the need to change, communicating this need, and accomplishing necessary incremental changes through the actions of employees. To align and communicate leadership expectations and responsibilities, terms such as vision, values and mission help get the attention of organizational employees to spark a desire for embracing progress.

Attaining organizational results requires visionary thinking and planning on multiple levels.

Visionary Thinking Places Employees' Best Interests First

Above everything else, the key to successfully implementing vision-related initiatives is for leaders to create positive environments for employees that allow them to embrace their unique talents and capabilities, feel secure, grow and prosper. Imparting the larger picture to employees in regard to organizational vision is one of the most effective tools for facilitating a solid commitment to new vision, values and mission. With commitment comes positive and enthusiastic action.

If employees "feel" secure about the promise of the vision and the importance of the mission they will begin to take ownership of them. "Feelings" are associated with the organizational values and values, tend to define the culture. Therefore, leaders should consider how well the organizational culture is aligned with their vision, mission and actions.

Visionary Thinking Focuses on Values

Values are what are most important in relationship to attaining leadership and organizational vision. They provide organizational as well as personal parameters and boundaries, and help to guide behavior, prioritize decisions, and justify the rationale for vision-related decisions. With organizational values as a foundation, vision is where the organization needs to go.

One of vision's main functions is to provide excitement about the mission or destination. Visional communication that is value-based explains to employees how all the various vision-related elements come together and interlink to determine actions that accomplish the desired goals, objectives and changes.

Vision and Positive Workplace Culture

Culture and leadership are often considered two sides of the same coin. This is because leaders tend to first create positive cultures when they establish well-functioning and collaborative groups within their organizations and departments. Once these cultures exist, they determine the best criteria for moving their visional direction forward.

Incorporating cultural understanding into the "visional picture" and directional goals and objectives is essential to leading effectively. If organizational and workplace cultures become dysfunctional, leaders have to think of strategies that can be implemented to successfully manage transformational change in such a way that their employees can survive and cope with it. If leaders are conscious of the cultures in which they operate and function, those cultures will manage the desired changes.

Visionary Thinking Coordinates Resources

Vision, values and mission become the means by which leaders are able to guide, influence and educate their employees. Among these three factors, vision becomes the "magnetic field" that works to align people, efforts and resources, which tends to generate a desire to incorporate positive planning, action steps and motivation to achieve successful outcomes.

Visionary thinking focuses on the ways and means to coordinate employees and resources that will make necessary changes a reality. It considers interconnections between organizational values, vision, and mission that work to provide a new sense of direction or drive higher levels of performance. This forms the basis for determining where the organization needs to go and the changes that will help get it there. Visionary thinking helps to eliminate management processes, practices and procedures that tend to void or negate positive vision-related efforts, workforce momentum and work-related enthusiasm.

Visionary Thinking Should Not Be Confused with Strategic Planning

Leadership is based on change, and change is about thinking differently and being creative. Strategic planning void of visionary thinking is nothing more than a superficial to-do list and may not detail the more in-depth pursuits needed to accomplish the real desired outcomes.

When vision, values, and mission guide an organization's strategic direction, real change becomes the driving force for the development of specific goals and objectives. In this way, vision and values become more of a strategic plan than the created project plans that are developed to accomplish particular goals and objectives.

Leading vision-related change is typically considered to be a right-brain activity in which getting people to see the reasons why change is necessary and how to go about implementing it is the focus. Managing vision-related change is mostly a left-brain activity concerned with the "what's and how's" of action steps, and laying out a strategic course and direction.

Developing visionary thinking requires addressing and designing implementation procedures and practices around eight steps.

- Establishing an immediate sense of urgency;
- Creating a vision-oriented "guiding and directing" base of supporters;
- Developing a separate strategy and vision for each smaller part of the

whole;

- Communicating the vision of change;
- Empowering broad-based employee actions;
- Generating short-term wins and successes;
- Consolidating gains in order to generate further change;
- Imbedding new approaches, philosophies and practices into the organizational culture.

Taken in their entirety, these steps can be viewed from a sequential perspective, which moves from leading visionary change to managing it in order to complete sequential and incremental forward movement. The final four steps may be seen as forming a transition from "where we as a collaborative group need to go" to "how we're going to get there."

Visionary Thinking Leads to Action

Once the leader's vision is defined and communicated, the visionary thinking process becomes officially translated into action. Strategic planning becomes more of a programming activity to support the leader's visionary thinking. Within this context a leader can expect tension between leading and managing change.

Visionary thinking should provide a means to support the creation of a common focus. This is not to be confused with the development of a vision statement. A formalized vision statement may or may not provide the desired common focus and commitment for needed actions or changes.

When a leader's vision statement becomes "etched in stone," it may inhibit refocusing, redefining, and communicating a new sense of direction for achieving a different end result or seeking out new opportunities. Within the visionary thinking process it is more important to develop ways to "etch" the leader's vision in employees' minds and hearts, as well as to guide their behaviors and attitudes.

It is just as important to develop criteria that consistently provides for decision making and prioritization that will accomplish the organization's vision-related mission. Visionary thinking is about creating new categories for developing or grouping previously developed strategies. It needs to focus on defining functions and processes that take leaders beyond their normal comfort zones and limitations to view things from new perspectives and in new combinations.

Aligning vision with action should be the goal of vision-based thinking and strategic planning. Ultimately, aligning vision and action should move the organization in the desired direction.

POINTS TO PONDER — SOMETHING TO THINK ABOUT

1. How would you define the phrase, "Culture and leadership are often considered two sides of the same coin"?
2. At what point do you believe visionary thinking becomes transformed into real action?
3. In what ways do you think visionary thinking can impact and provide support for creating common focus among employees?

TRAINING ACTIVITY — APPLICATION & ACTION PLAN

Transform your visionary thinking into action through the following steps:

1. Determine whether your existing vision statement provides a common focus and commitment for needed actions or changes.
2. If it is not as effective for instilling positive employee actions as it should be, look for ways you can begin to refocus, redefine, and communicate a new sense of direction for achieving different end results.
3. Begin to look for ways to focus on new possibilities or opportunities as they relate to your visional direction.
4. Think of creative ways to etch your vision into your employees' minds and hearts.

5. Think about and incorporate strategies and methods that are able to guide their behaviors and attitudes.
6. Develop criteria that will consistently provide for decision making and prioritization that work to accomplish your organization's vision-related mission.
7. Create an overarching message and use it as an impetus for change.

6

Selling Your Vision

Before a vision can be attained, leaders need to "sell" it. Selling a vision implies generating employee buy-in and collective efforts to reach specific goals and objectives within it. In this pursuit, leaders present the vision in such a way that employees develop a desire to work toward attaining it. They integrate and implement employee ideas to foster ownership of the vision.

To move the vision forward, leaders speak in terms of dreams and possibilities, continually sharing the larger picture of how the vision relates to the total organization. They utilize all applicable employee talents, capabilities and abilities along the way, and continually gain understanding and input from all involved parties.

IMPLICATIONS — WHAT THIS MEANS TO YOU

Vision helps employees and leaders make sound decisions, because they are made with the end result very much in the forefront of their minds. This is why it is crucial for a leader to sell the vision at every available opportunity.

Vision takes into account a larger picture than the immediate goal. Selling it takes powerful and specific images that form the values of the organization, including respect and consideration for all involved employee members. It must continue to mobilize and guide employees beyond normal limits and expectations.

Selling a vision is about going somewhere and taking the organization and its employees along on the journey. It creates a long-term, proactive stance that allows leaders to generate desired results, rather than a short-term, reactive stance that simply seeks to rid the workplace and organization of undesirable practices or elements.

Selling a vision needs to reveal what business the company is in, as well as its core reason or purpose for existence. Focused on generating organizational energy, the process stresses broad guidelines for how to go about fulfilling the organization's purpose—including a clear picture of what specifically defines success.

If a leader's organizational vision is compelling, employees will think their work worthwhile and become both more happily and purposefully engaged in it.

Selling the 'Picture of the Future'

A picture of the future is the vision's end result. It is important to outline this future picture of the organization according to what it will look like in its purpose, functions, opportunities and possibilities. The picture should focus only on this end result and not the process of getting there.

In order to effectively sell this larger picture of the future, a leader cannot be vague in describing its associated benefits, possibilities and opportunities. It should be something tangible and concrete that employees as well as leaders can actually "see" and relate to.

Selling a vision is much more than simply embellishing and gloating over possible accomplishments and likely positive outcomes. A sold vision is put into action, not simply talked about. For example, Walt Disney's picture of the future was expressed in the mandatory charge he gave every cast member to "keep the same smile on people's faces when they leave the park as when they entered." He was not interested in whether guests were in the park 2 hours or 10: his organizational purpose was focused on being in the "happiness business," and as such he was going to keep them smiling.

Selling the Vision Helps Make It a Reality

The most important components in the process of effectively promoting a vision is how it is creatively detailed, communicated and translated into actions. If a leader is honest about present realities and clear about their vision, things will begin to take shape and start happening of their own accord.

As it is essential to allow employees to help shape the vision by placing their personal imprint upon it, the process encourages dialogue. This will deepen their understanding and commitment as well as create a vision that can be better attained with less hindrances and resistance.

In order for leadership efforts to make a difference and have a long-lasting impact, it is critical to redefine and reinforce exactly where the leader and employees are going by selling the vision. As problems obviously occur when no one knows what they are supposed to be doing, all within the organization need to know what their purpose is, what they are trying to accomplish, and even how they are expected to behave when working according to the vision's purpose and direction. In the absence of a clearly and effectively sold vision, an organization becomes nothing more than a self-serving bureaucracy.

Once the vision is sold to the point where it becomes accepted and embraced, the leader can focus on serving and being more responsive to employee's needs and concerns.

Some of the greatest leaders throughout history were able to mobilize others by selling people on a shared vision. Louis Gerstner Jr. took the helm of IBM in 1993 amid turmoil and instability as the company's annual net losses reached a record $8 billion. Gerstner was initially quoted as saying, "The last thing IBM needs is a vision." However, less than a year later he acknowledged that IBM badly needed long-range planning. It became clear that the focus of strength for the company would lie in integrated solutions. As a result of that clarity, Gerstner resisted pressure to split the company, and an incredible turnaround was effected.

In 1995, delivering the keynote address at the computer industry trade show, Gerstner articulated IBM's new vision—that network computing would drive the next phase of industry growth and would be the company's overarching strategy. That year, IBM began a series of acquisitions that positioned services to become the fastest growing segment of the company, with annual growth at more than 20%.

Selling a Vision Means Empowering Employees

A compelling organizational vision will help employees think less about themselves and more about working collectively as a positive, unified force. Through actively and effectively selling a vision, employees should begin to share and believe in what the organization can be, and because of it, typically begin to generate tremendous synergized energy and excitement.

Selling a vision makes employees feel they are making a difference. Knowing exactly what they are expected to do and why, they begin to desire building a strong reputation for excellent work ethics, products and services. A strong sense of trust and respect is established. Because they understand that everyone will end up sharing accountability, employees assume higher levels of responsibility, and begin to see more clearly how to work toward their personal as well as organizational goals and direction.

If a vision is sold properly, all individual employees will want to assume responsibility for their own actions. When this desire takes root, they will also tend to take charge of their future rather than passively waiting for it to happen.

Within the process of selling their vision, leaders need to make room for inventiveness, trial and error, creativity and risk taking, since these work to effectively inspire employees to higher levels of achievement. In this manner, employees can make their contributions in their own way, and their differences are respected since everyone knows they are in the same boat together, where all are part of a larger "whole picture" and are forging new paths into the future.

POINTS TO PONDER – SOMETHING TO THINK ABOUT

1. Do you believe a properly sold vision will induce individual employees to assume responsibility for their own actions? Why or why not?
2. In what ways do you think selling a vision works to reinforce and redefine where leaders and employees are going and how?
3. How does vision buy-in help employees and leaders make better decisions?

TRAINING ACTIVITY – APPLICATION & ACTION PLAN

Develop a plan for effectively selling your vision by incorporating the following action steps:

1. Integrate and implement employee ideas to move the vision forward.
2. Present your vision in such a way that employees develop a desire to work towards attaining it.
3. Detail and apply various employee talents, capabilities and abilities in the vision attainment process, as well as to maintain their sense of ownership in the vision itself.
4. Infuse dreams and possibilities into your visional descriptions and details in order to better inspire specific goal and objective attainment.
5. Detail specific ideas that can energize employees to embrace their own vision of the future.
6. Focus on gaining input from all involved parties that are needed to fulfill the vision, and share these with other leaders and managers.
7. Continually share your vision's "big picture" as it relates to the total organization's mission and values.

7

Why Vision Is Essential

Vision enables anticipating and reacting to the future, and better positioning of the business, by defining where both the competition and customer are going. Essential for infusing organizational cultures with the motivational impetus and collaborative efforts, the vision's structures and guidelines help translate directional choices into action.

Defining a vision is important because organizational leaders are induced to determine their own individual philosophies, which are then translated into directional courses of action. This philosophy ends up clarifying what choices are necessary for achieving the vision within their particular organizational setting.

Generating real changes that reflect mutual interests and benefits, a vision eliminates the need to demand, command and control employees. This common purpose makes for dynamic relationships between leaders and collaborators. All in the organization are moved to higher levels of motivation and moral development, which in essence is its real, intended purpose.

IMPLICATIONS – WHAT THIS MEANS TO YOU

Vision in its truest sense is the art of influencing employees by persuasion or example to follow a line of action. It must never be used as a means to compel employees through intimidation or force to follow a line of action. Vision defines the activities needed for a leader to influence employees to cooperate toward a goal they have come to see as desirable. It induces them to act in accordance with the company's values in pursuit of its overall good.

STRATEGIES, TIPS & TECHNIQUES TO APPLY

Leaders may not feel comfortable saying, "All we have in this organization is each other." This is why they have a vision: it communicates this important reality for them. The more people begin to recognize and understand it, the more work assignment goals take on a deeper meaning, and specific purposes and employee synergy drive them to completion.

Vision begins the quest for organizational authenticity and collective unity. It establishes the criteria for anticipating and altering the future, and is essential for creating the open space and anticipatory "story" that encourages organizational shifts in methods and operations, creative thinking and the pursuit of opportunities.

Vision Fosters Leadership Courage by Demanding Answers to Vital Questions

Leaders do not move the organization, employees and themselves forward by not facing the facts about the business and the environment in which it is operating. This means answering fundamental questions regarding the company, work environment, competition and customer:

- Where as a company are we most vulnerable?
- As a division or department?
- What does the landscape of the competitive environment say about where future trends, the competition and the customer are headed?
- What company values, beliefs and principles are being threatened and must be preserved?
- How does my vision fit within the larger organizational picture?
- Where is the leadership in my organization, and does it reflect a purpose similar to mine?

- What specific actions can my vision influence to unify efforts and help the organization move steadily toward its mission and goals?
- Will my vision generate or overcome resistance to change within the organization?
- How can my vision help bring employees' unique talents and perspectives to the table and encourage and reward their efforts?

While these questions will often uncover unpleasant realities, meeting them head-on will create a renewed sense of fortitude and perseverance to overcome and move beyond them.

Vision Strengthens Organizational Commitment

Vision tends to reflect itself in a leader's commitment to be an example by "walking the talk." Its bottom line within an organization begins with clarity in leadership communication, assertions and action. This then demonstrates the leader's integrity, which initiates a chain reaction of increased sense of workplace purpose, motivation and accomplishment.

Vision allows traditional norms, structures and even some values to lose their binding power as the rules of cooperation become reinvented. A culture of commitment and accountability repeatedly emerges in visional pictures and narratives. Tasks tend to become personal challenges and mastered as individual achievements. Vision plays an integral part in establishing joy and delight in creating, shaping and framing problems, challenges and solutions.

Vision Establishes a Personal and Emotional Connection to Tasks and Assignments

Vision-led leadership is the art of influencing employees through persuasion, which tends to be accomplished through a hands on approach to problem solving and assignment completion.

Vision through example should never be confused with "drivership," or compelling employees to follow a particular line of action through intimidation. It actively influences employees to cooperate toward a corporate goal they have come to perceive as desirable. Vision becomes the inspiration and mobilization of everyone to undertake collective action in pursuit of the common organizational good. Through vision the capability of employees to fulfill a purpose through the development of character becomes maximized. Without vision it becomes impossible for organizations to confront problems whose solutions require the unified focus of everyone in the work environment.

POINTS TO PONDER – SOMETHING TO THINK ABOUT

1. Why from a personal standpoint do you feel vision is essential to the organization?
2. How would you go about defining your vision to another organizational member?

TRAINING ACTIVITY – APPLICATION & ACTION PLAN

Vision is one of the most oft-used but least understood terms in business. To help incorporate a detailed vision for your organization, apply the following strategies.

1. Define your organization's fundamental reason for existence beyond just generating capital.
2. Detail your organization's core values.
3. List what you believe are large, yet ultimately achievable, possibilities for your organization's future.
4. Define these possibilities as likely attainable goals.
5. Formulate these into an initial vision statement that you can further reflect upon, modify and refine.

8

Communicating Your Vision

Vision communication can be thought of as expressing an ideal that represents or reflects the organization's collectively shared values. Numerous studies have shown that leaders who enthusiastically promote and communicate their vision tend to create positive effects on employee performance, attitudes and perceptions.

Specific core components need to be incorporated to effectively communicate one's vision. These are:

- Displaying a charismatic, forceful, animated and confident communication style;
- Taking action to support the implementation of the vision, such as by serving as an exemplary role model;
- Intellectually stimulating employees and building their confidence while continuously promoting the vision.

IMPLICATIONS — WHAT THIS MEANS TO YOU

A well thought-out vision concisely but openly expresses a leader's values and energy. In this way, vision content is communicated through imagery that generates a vivid mental picture of possibilities in relationship to existing realities.

STRATEGIES, TIPS & TECHNIQUES TO APPLY

When communicating their vision, leaders should focus on detailing its strategic emphasis and response to necessary changes. This includes outlining expectations as to the vision's degree of control over those changes and its relationship to employees' self-interests, as well as combining specific needs and values into a unified and collaborative effort.

Describing the Vision in Terms of Mission, Values and Goals

Communicating a vision effectively needs to incorporate components of the leader's organizational mission, strategy, values and goals. Leaders need to communicate the vision in such a way as to integrate all these elements and place them into a visual framework that works to guide future action. Communicating a vision needs to motivate the setting of specific task-related goals, which in turn affect and alter performance.

It is essential to maintain clarity when communicating visional direction, with goals specifically detailed and explained. As part of this communication process, statements should include imagery that is specifically related to:

- Performance
- Achievement and improvement
- Future time perspectives
- Assumptions of personal responsibility
- Initiatives and their acceptance
- Anticipating future possibilities

Goals should be described in desirable terms that reflect ways to address challenges or the future orientation of the organization. For example, results-focused company goals may become the equivalent of task-specific targets such as "doubling production output within the next two years."

The Importance of Modeling the Vision

While effective communication of a vision has a direct and obvious effect on performance, it is more likely to generate indirect impacts on motivation, acceptance, and perseverance in overcoming challenges and hindrances. Indirect positive results are realized when employees know the purpose behind the vision's structure and understand its content, attributes and interrelationships from their own personal perspective.

As simply communicating a well-formulated vision is not enough to guarantee results, leaders within the organization must "walk the talk." As part of the communication process, leaders need to reinforce the vision's inherent values through consistent and animated positive role modeling as well as in the way they select and work with employees, acknowledge small changes and reward successes.

Vision Needs Visibility

Leaders often tend to articulate a vision taken straight from their organization's strategic plan or their own personal planning process. When doing this, they begin to rewrite a modified or restructured vision and mission statement, or sometimes even find themselves devising and establishing an altogether new set of organizational values. Most times these efforts only muddy the visional communication process and leave employees confused. This in turn results in hindering the goals they desire to pursue, and effective ways to achieve them.

Communication of a vision does not rely on the underlying rationale as much as it does on making exciting possibilities "visible" within the organization. Leaders can accomplish this by openly communicating and stressing the following:

- Inspiring with a sense of passion;
- Employee well-being as a direct benefit of the vision;
- Vision as an adaptive tool for organizational and group survival;
- The necessity of building and maintaining work effectiveness;
- Courage and a willingness to take a stand;
- The rewards of ambition and perseverance;
- Integrity, ethics and values;
- Generating self-esteem and emotional stability;

- Developing patience, endurance and tolerance for ambiguity;
- Quality decision making;
- The importance of stimulating creative thinking and innovation;
- The intention to utilize all employees' functional, technical and organizational skills in pursuit of the vision;
- Priority setting as a necessary tool to accomplish assignments, projects and tasks in a timely and effective manner.

To align and communicate vision-related responsibilities, leaders utilize terms related to organizational values and mission, exciting challenges, unified efforts, and work-related incentives to help get the attention of employees. Doing this makes the vision concrete and tangible, and sets in motion key elements for reaching the necessary goals that steadily lead to its attainment.

POINTS TO PONDER — SOMETHING TO THINK ABOUT

1. Do you tend to display a charismatic, forceful, animated and confident communication style? Why or why not?
2. What does the statement "Vision content needs to be communicated through imagery" imply?

TRAINING ACTIVITY — APPLICATION & ACTION PLAN

Apply the following concepts and points of emphasis to create a powerful message that reflects your visional content and direction.

1. Describing as vividly as possible your vision's strategic emphasis.
2. Detail your vision's response to necessary organizational change.
3. Define how your vision intends to control and manage elements of change.

4. Linking your vision to employees' self-interests.
5. Addressing and aligning specific needs and values in relationship to collaborative efforts and a sense of workplace unity.
6. Good role modeling techniques including an animated and consistently positive personal attitude.
7. Acknowledging verbal employee input and praising small successes.

About the Author

Timothy F. Bednarz, Ph.D. is CEO of the American Management Development Group, Inc. For over 20 years he has researched, designed and authored hundreds of learning and development programs used by Fortune 1000 companies.

He is also the author of *Great! What Makes Leaders Great. What They Did, How They Did It and What You Can Learn from It* (2011).

Speaking Availability

Timothy F. Bednarz, Ph.D. is available for speaking engagements for your next meeting or association event. He can be contacted at 800-654-4935 or by e-mail at timothy.bednarz@majorium.com.

Bulk Sales

Bulk sales of this book or any other titles available from Majorium Business Press. Inquiries can be directed to sales@majorium.com, or by phone at 800-6654-4935.

Quick Order Form

Fax orders: 715-342-1118. Send this form.

Telephone orders: Call 800-654-4935 toll-free. Have your credit card ready.

Email orders: sales@majorium.com

Postal orders: Majorium Business Press, 2025 Main Street, Stevens Point, WI 54481, USA.

Please send the following books:

____

____

____

____

Please send more FREE information on:

❑Catalog ❑Speaking/Seminars ❑Mailing Lists ❑Consulting

Name: ____________________________________

Address: __________________________________

City: ____________________ State: _____ Zip: _________

Telephone: ________________________________

Email address: _____________________________

Sales tax: Please add 5.5% for products shipped to Wisconsin addresses.

Shipping by air:

United States: $4.00 for first book and $2.00 for each additional product.

International: $9.00 for first book; $5.00 for each additional product (estimate).

Made in United States
Cleveland, OH
06 November 2026

47678344R10037